PETER RABBIT 2

QUIZ BOOK

PUFFIN

MEET THE STARS

Howdy fans! Let's say 'hello' to Peter and his co-stars and get ready for a hop-tastic adventure.

We start Peter's next adventure with a wedding, and there's one member of this delightful bunch that really stands out. But it isn't the bride. It's **Peter Rabbit!**

PETER

BENJAMIN

FLOPSY

MOPSY

COTTON-TAIL

BEA AND THOMAS

PETER RABBIT

Give it up for the one, the only ... Peter Rabbit!

Let me tell you a bit about Peter Rabbit. He's cheeky, he's funny and he's Mischievous with a capital M. Sometimes, he simply can't help getting into trouble as things just sort of happen around him. (Sometimes, things are 100% his fault.)

Peter Rabbit lives in a place so beautiful that it belongs on a postcard. In fact, it is on a postcard – lots and lots of postcards. Peter is lucky enough to live near Lake Windermere in the Lake District, with his sisters Flopsy, Mopsy and Cotton-tail, and his cousin Benjamin.

Peter loves vegetables – the fresher the better. If they are plucked straight from the vegetable patch and eaten right away, then those are the best vegetables of all. Once, Peter and his fellow rabbits used to steal vegetables from their neighbour, Mr. McGregor, but that's all history. Now, there are no gates on the garden. The rabbits can take anything they like ... as long as it's not one of Mr. McGregor's precious tomatoes.

Cheekiness:	10	Enthusiasm:	10
Courage:	10	Naughtiness:	10
Cleverness:	10	Sense of humour:	10

LIKES:
All vegetables, Benjamin Bunny, Flopsy, Mopsy, Cotton-tail and Bea.

FAMOUS FOR:
Going on tremendously dangerous and ever so scary adventures.

10 THINGS YOU NEED TO KNOW ABOUT PETER RABBIT!

1 He's a great big brother.

2 The blue jacket he wears used to belong to his father.

3 A long time ago, his father was put in a pie by Mrs. McGregor.

4 He misses his father dreadfully.

5 He LOVES Bea.

 6 Once, he and Thomas McGregor were deadly enemies.

 7 They are still not terribly fond of each other, but they are trying to get along.

 **8** He does his very, very best to be super cool.

 9 But he can't help acting the fool to make others laugh.

 10 Sometimes, however, everything that he touches goes wrong . . .

PETER'S JOKES

Peter can't help telling a joke! Here are some of his favourites.

Q: What do you call a fox with Mr. McGregor's squashed tomatoes in his ears?

A: Anything you like – it can't hear you!

Q: What do you call a rabbit that's been out in the sun too long?

A: A hot cross bunny.

Q: What does Peter Rabbit say before he and his fellow rabbits tuck into a salad?

A: Lettuce eat!

Q: What's Peter Rabbit's favourite kind of dance music?

A: Hip-hop.

Use this page to make up your own jokes.

WEDDING WHEEL

Now that Bea and Thomas are married, Peter and Mr. McGregor get along . . . most of the time. Can you work out Peter's message for Thomas?

Use the code wheel to help you!

PETER'S MESSAGE

| 6 | 1 | 13 | 9 | 12 | 25 |

___ ___ ___ ___ ___ ___

CHARACTER CONFUSION

These characters names have all been scrambled!
Solve the scrambles and then use the bold letters
to find out which rabbit star we're about to meet!

BASANBRA

_ _ _ _ _ _ _ _

RPT**EE**

_ _ _ _ _

GPLI**N**GI LNABD

_ _ _ _ _ _ _ _ _ _ _ _

M**J**EAMI LPDEUD-UKDC

_ _ _ _ _ _ _ _ _ _ _ - _ _ _ _

ATOSHM

_ _ _ _ _ _

P**M**YOS

_ _ _ _ _

SRM. **GI**GYT-WIKELN

_ _ _ . _ _ _ _ _ - _ _ _ _ _ _

TCTO**N**O-ATLI

_ _ _ _ _ _ - _ _ _ _

We're about to meet:

_ _ _ _ _ _ _ _ _

13

BENJAMIN BUNNY

He's a sidekick in a million!

Whether his cousin Peter Rabbit is stuck in a sticky situation or ready for an adventure, Benjamin Bunny is always there to help out. He's pretty good at giving advice too, on account of being super sensible and very, very wise. If you want to know the answer to anything, ask Benjamin Bunny.

Cheekiness:	2	Enthusiasm:	9
Courage:	7	Naughtiness:	3
Cleverness:	6	Sense of humour:	6

LIKES:
Onions, tomatoes and raw vegetables.

FAMOUS FOR:
Helping Peter Rabbit rescue his blue jacket from Mr. McGregor's garden.

ODD ONE OUT

Circle the odd character out in each row.

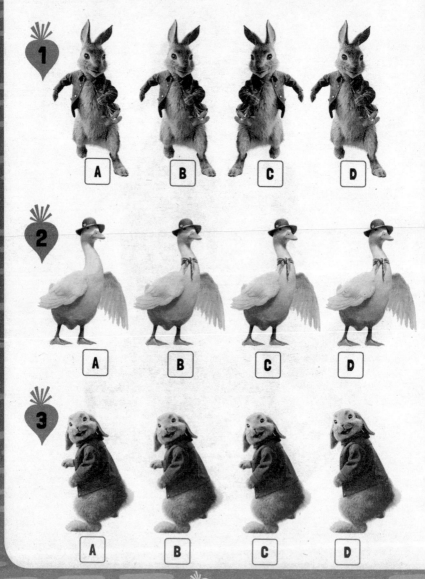

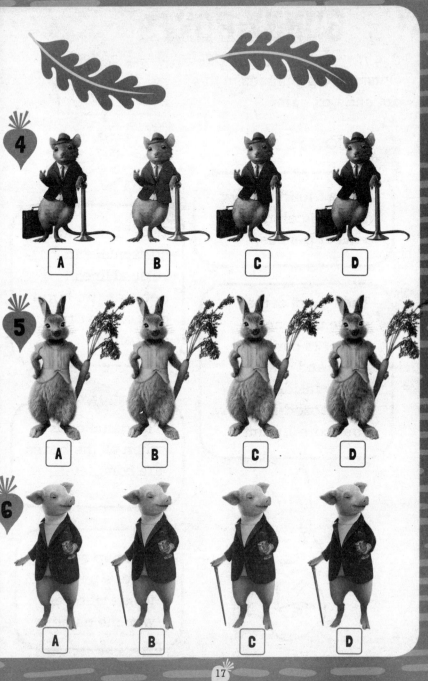

4

A B C D

5

A B C D

6

A B C D

BUNNY BOXES

Outsmart the bunnies in this dot and box game.

HOW TO PLAY:

1 Find a friend and two different-coloured pens or pencils.

2 Take turns drawing horizontal and vertical lines between two large dots on the grid opposite.

3 The object of the game is for each player to complete a box and draw a bunny inside it. For each boxed-in bunny, you score 1 point.

4 The game ends when all the boxes are complete.

5 Add up each player's bunnies to see who has won the game!

SCORE SHEET		
PLAYER		
POINTS		

10 THINGS YOU NEED TO KNOW ABOUT PETER RABBIT'S SISTERS!

1 Flopsy, Mopsy and Cotton-tail are triplets.

2 Peter Rabbit is their big brother.

3 Everyone thinks that Flopsy and Mopsy look alike (because they do).

4 Flopsy is so fed up of being confused with Mopsy that she changes her name to something that doesn't rhyme. So she calls herself Lavatory! (If only she knew what 'lavatory' meant . . .)

5 Flopsy and Mopsy do not like sparkling water.

6 Cotton-tail likes jellybeans a little too much.

7 Bea's publisher has a name for Flopsy and Mopsy – the Dynamic Duo. Meanwhile, Cotton-tail is nicknamed the Firecracker.

8 They are very well-behaved . . . most of the time.

9 They are big softies and adore their big brother.

10 They are always ready for adventure!

BOTHER IN GLOUCESTER

Peter is in a spot of bother. Can you help him find his way to his family without bumping into Barnabas's gang? Mark their hiding spots on the grid, using these clues. For each one, begin at the start. Then draw a safe route for Peter through Gloucester.

1 SAMUEL WHISKERS
Go right four spaces and up three spaces.

2 TOM KITTEN
Head up four spaces.

3 MITTENS
Move right two spaces and up six spaces.

4 BARNABAS
Go up five spaces and skip to the right three spaces.

HOME

START

DOODLE PETER

Can you doodle a doppelgänger
for Peter in four easy steps?

1 Draw a potato shape for his face.

2 Add two carrot shapes for ears.

3 Draw on two large eyes and a bunny nose.

4 Doodle some whiskers and a mouth.

BOUNCING BUNNIES

How many of each bunny can you count on the page? Which bunny features the most? Turn the page to read all about this movie-star character!

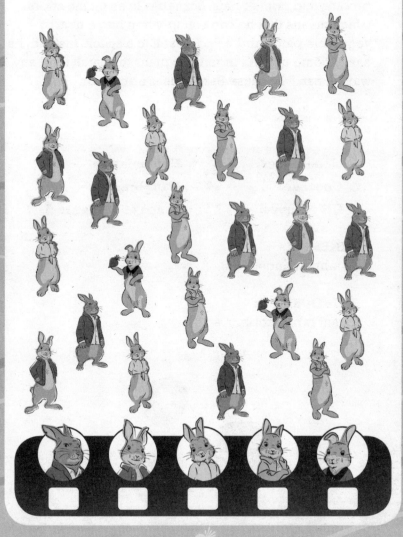

BARNABAS

Barnabas is gruff, he's rough and he's tough.

He's also exceedingly good at dodging pepper spray, brooms and cricket bats. Barnabas lives on the streets, which means that he can't simply hop into a nearby vegetable patch and help himself to a snack. Instead, he has to come up with ingenious plans to snatch food any way he can – because Barnabas is a survivor.

Cheekiness:	6	Enthusiasm:	5
Courage:	10	Naughtiness:	10
Cleverness:	8	Sense of humour:	3

LIKES:
Stealing things.

FAMOUS FOR:
Great rabbit robberies.

BUNNY BOOKMARK

Keep Barnabas's gang away from your quiz book with this bunny bookmark.

YOU WILL NEED

- A piece of card
- Scissors
- A pen or pencil
- Glue
- Colouring pens

INSTRUCTIONS:

1. Cut out the bookmark template opposite.

2. Draw some bunny ears at the top of your bookmark.

3. Cut around the ears and fold one over, half-way down.

4. Add a bunny face to your bookmark.

5. Write 'Top Secret' on the bottom of the bookmark.

6. Stick your bookmark on to a piece of card and cut around it to make it sturdy.

7. Colour your bunny bookmark however you like.

8. Place your bookmark in this book, folding one ear over the top of the page.

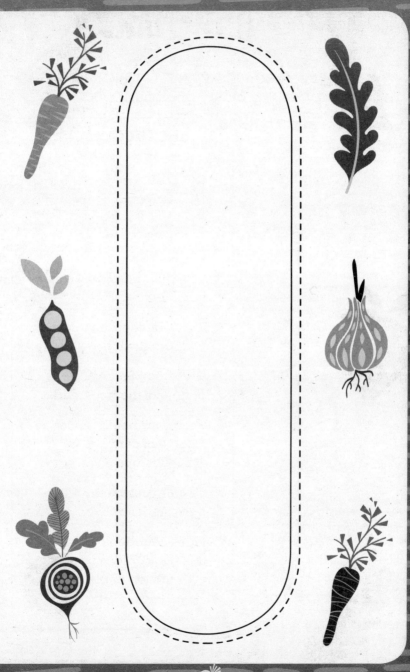

BARNABAS'S GANG

SAMUEL WHISKERS is a rat in a tweed jacket. He might look as adorable as a favourite uncle but don't be fooled. He really isn't. He's a top thief.

TOM KITTEN and his sister **MITTENS** are two stylish kittens who always look out for each other – when they're not busy being rotten thieves, that is.

MYSTERY MAZE

Peter and his sisters have had enough of the city. They want to get back home.

Can you help them find their way through the maze and back to Bea's cottage?

START

FINISH

IN THE SHADE

The gang are a shady bunch! Can you identify the gang members from their shadows?

1

2

3

4

Samuel Whiskers

Mittens

Tom Kitten

Barnabas

10 THINGS YOU NEED TO KNOW ABOUT BEA AND THOMAS

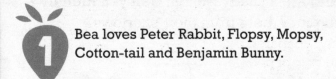

1 Bea loves Peter Rabbit, Flopsy, Mopsy, Cotton-tail and Benjamin Bunny.

2 She also loves Thomas McGregor.

3 Thomas loves Bea.

4 He is s-l-o-w-l-y getting used to Bea's rabbit family.

5 Bea and Thomas are newly-weds. Hip hip hooray! Everyone throw confetti!

34

6

Bea is always prepared to believe the best of people and animals.

7

Thomas loves tomatoes. If anyone touches his tomatoes, it makes him very, very, very, very, very, VERY cross indeed.

8

He now runs his very own toyshop.

9

Thomas has turned Bea's words and pictures into a beautiful book.

10

Bea is a wonderful storyteller. She writes about her beloved Peter Rabbit and her animal friends. Her bunny illustrations are simply stunning.

A TALE OF BOBTAILS

Create your own Peter Rabbit tale, just like Bea,
and add some twists here and there! Circle two items
from each section and use them in your story.

HEROES

Peter, Bea, Benjamin, Johnny Town-mouse,
Mrs. Tiggy-winkle, Flopsy, Mopsy and Cotton-tail

BADDIES

Nigel Basil-Jones, Barnabas, Samuel Whiskers,
Tom Kitten, Mr. and Mrs. McGregor

SETTINGS

Garden, city, lake, toyshop, museum,
circus, houseboat, garden centre

OBJECTS

Vegetables, jacket, book, mobile phone,
backpack, glasses, sneakers

THREATS

Bad bunny, busy road, crook, pet shop, train journey

TRIUMPHS

Escape, beat the baddie,
outwit someone, steal
vegetables, befriend a new
character, learn something
about yourself

SURPRISES

Be rescued by
an unexpected character,
surprise party, chase scene,
argument, find treasure

THE REST OF THE CAST

Peter Rabbit 2 isn't all about rabbits, you know! There are all sorts of wildlife to meet . . .

Mrs. Tiggy-winkle might have prickles – she's a hedgehog, after all – but she doesn't have a prickly personality. She's kinder than kind and super brave, too.

Pigling Bland is a great fan of food. All food. Given half a chance, he will eat anything and everything. And then go back for seconds. And probably thirds too.

Mr. Tod is a quick-thinking, clever fox. If you see him, be warned – he's a trickster who loves nothing better than fooling others.

Tommy Brock is a totally trustworthy badger. Unbelievably, he has something in common with Thomas McGregor. They both love tomatoes.

Jemima Puddle-duck is easy to spot because she wears a beautiful bonnet. (And she's a duck, of course.) She's kind, caring and a little bit silly.

Jeremy Fisher is at home on land and on water – because he's a frog! He's very reliable. If you're going to take a frog on an adventure, pick Jeremy Fisher. You won't regret it.

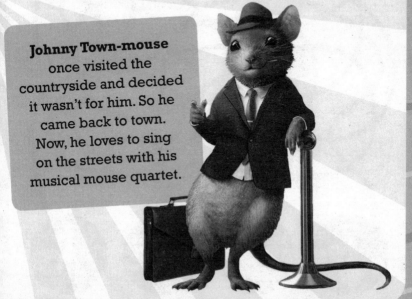

Johnny Town-mouse once visited the countryside and decided it wasn't for him. So he came back to town. Now, he loves to sing on the streets with his musical mouse quartet.

RADISH RUN

Peter wants to munch on a radish. Circle the path that takes Peter to the yummy snack.

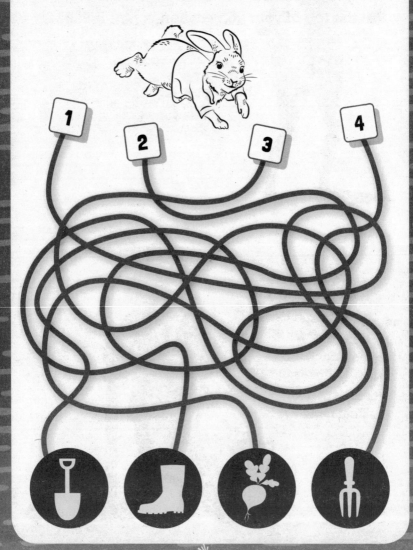

A BRAND NEW DAY

JW Rooster II needs to wake the rest of the animals. Quickly draw the sun rising as fast as you can and shout 'cock-a-doodle-doo' at the top of your voice when you're finished!

COCK-A-DOODLE-DOO!

RABBIT RAVE

The animals know how to get down and boogie!
Here's how to have your own animal riot and throw
your own *Peter Rabbit* party!

DECORATIONS

- Draw and cut out lots of rabbit shapes.
  Punch holes in the tops of the ears
  and string them together to make
  some bunny bunting.

- Buy some cotton wool and stick bunny
  tails on to your guests' cups and plates.

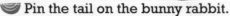

PARTY GAMES

- Pin the tail on the bunny rabbit.
- Do the bunny hop!
- Perform some magic and pull a
  bunny out of a hat!
- Make your guests their own bunny
  mask to take home.
- Hop, skip and bob to music for
  as long as you like!

PARTY FOOD

* Why, lots of vegetables of course! Arrange your veg. in a rainbow of colours for added WOW factor!

* Look up a recipe for a vegetable cake, such as beetroot and chocolate cake.

Delicious!

* Blend lots of delicious fruit and vegetables together to make a smoothie that no bunny can possibly resist.

THE PERFECTLY HUGE
PETER RABBIT QUIZ

How much do you really know about Peter Rabbit?
Use your knowledge to answer these fiendishly
difficult questions. Choose a), b) or c).

1 What happened to Peter's father?

a) He ran away to Spain.

b) He was put in a pie.

c) He became a world high-jump champion.

Answer

2 **What are Peter's triplet sisters called?**

Answer

a) Flopsy, Mopsy and Popsy.

b) Lavatory, Sink and Bath.

c) Flopsy, Mopsy and Cotton-tail.

3 **Who was once Peter's mortal enemy?**

Answer

a) Mr. McGregor.

b) Mr. McDougal.

c) Mr. McDonald.

4 **What else does Nigel Basil-Jones call Peter?**

Answer ☐

a) The Rotten Egg.

b) The Bad Seed.

c) The Squashed Tomato.

5 **Why does Peter run away to the city?**

Answer ☐

a) He wants to see the sights.

b) He's heard that the streets are paved with gold.

c) He feels terribly upset when he's portrayed as the villain in Bea's new book and wants to get away from everyone.

6 **Peter makes a lot of . . .?**

a) Pies.

b) Sticky toffee puddings.

c) Mistakes.

Answer ☐

7 **If Peter were given this menu, which meal would he choose?**

Answer

a) A massive plate of vegetables.

b) A fancy soup with croutons.

c) A complicated dessert with cream and jam.

8 **Peter absolutely adores one person. Who?**

Answer

a) Mr. McGregor.

b) Bea.

c) Nigel Basil-Jones.

Mr. McGregor

Bea

Nigel Basil-Jones

WHAT'S MISSING?

Can you fill in the missing words in this cautionary tale about an exceedingly cool rabbit?

Meet Peter Rabbit! He's .... ,

he's funny and he's terribly good at pinching

.... Unfortunately, he's not that

great at recognizing when others are telling

....

Take .... , for instance. He's

.... , through and through.

But he convinces poor Peter to swap

the beautiful .... for a life

of crime in the big ....

And before he knows it, Peter is involved

in a .... to steal a huge amount

of produce from a farmers' ....

Will he see the .... of his ways

in time? Or will it be too late . . . ?

Barnabas   error

carrots   fibs

cheeky   market

city   plot

countryside   rotten

BEA'S QUIZ

She's beautiful inside and out. But how much do you really know about Peter Rabbit's most favourite human ever?

 1 What does Bea love to do?

a) Flamenco dancing.

b) Painting and writing.

c) Painting and decorating.

Answer

2 Bea pretends to have read every single book that one famous author has written. Which autho

a) J. K. Rowling.

b) Philip Pullman.

c) Charles Dickens.

Answer

3 In Bea's stories, who are the main characters?

a) The rabbits.

b) Mrs. Tiggy-winkle.

c) Thomas McGregor.

Answer

4 When she gets married, does Bea keep her own surname?

a) She's decided to change it to Mrs. Rabbit.

b) Of course! It's the twenty-first century, don't you know.

c) She's always longed to be a Mrs. and changed it to McGregor immediately.

Answer

BENJAMIN'S TOP TIPS

Benjamin is a wise rabbit with plenty of advice. But can you spot which of these tips belong to Benjamin and which are totally made up?

TRUE or FALSE

1. Look at a fixed point on the horizon when travelling to avoid feeling sick. ☐ ☐

2. Soup boils, soup spoils. Simmer it instead! ☐ ☐

3. Vegetables in the shape of rectangles are amazing! ☐ ☐

4. Buy cheap, buy twice. ☐ ☐

5. Never trust a dodgy rabbit. ☐ ☐

6. A bird in the hand is worth two in the bush. ☐ ☐

7. Never a borrower nor a lender be. ☐ ☐

8. More haste less speed. ☐ ☐

9. Eating too much sugar makes a rabbit thirsty. ☐ ☐

10. The proof of the pudding is in the eating. ☐ ☐

NIGEL BASIL-JONES

Fill in the missing words in this article about top publisher, **Mr. Nigel Basil-Jones**.

Meet Nigel Basil-Jones, the publisher! He is very handsome and super ....
His fancy office is .... , its shelves lined with many, many ....

Nigel is incredibly charming to all of his .... Take the delightful .... , for example. He makes sure to .... her hand when he meets her.

And he creates a wonderful area where Bea's .... family can ....
As Nigel is so enormously .... , he is sure that he can turn Bea's new book into a .... All she has to do is change it, just a little.

authors	kiss
Bea	confident
bestseller	rabbit
books	relax
gigantic	successful

PLOT TWIST!

Nigel Basil-Jones has big plans for Bea's book and she makes a lot of changes to keep him happy. In the new version, which of the following are true and which are false?

TRUE or FALSE

1 Pigling Bland speaks Russian. ☐ ☐

2 Flopsy is a superhero. ☐ ☐

3 Mopsy is a corporate lawyer. ☐ ☐

4 Cotton-tail wins a talent competition. ☐ ☐

5 Peter Rabbit is a bad guy. ☐ ☐

6 The rabbits are sent into space in a rocket ship. ☐ ☐

7 The rabbits enter a jam-making competition. ☐ ☐

8 Peter Rabbit breaks the world land speed record. ☐ ☐

9 The rabbits play ukuleles. ☐ ☐

FLOPSY, MOPSY AND COTTON-TAIL

How much do you know about Peter's sisters. Complete the quiz to test your knowledge.

1 **Who is *really* the oldest triplet?**

a) Flopsy.

b) Mopsy.

c) Cotton-tail.

Answer

2 **What does Nigel Basil-Jones call Flopsy and Mopsy?**

a) The Pretty Pair.

b) The Dynamic Duo.

c) The Cute Couple.

Answer

3 **And what does Nigel Basil-Jones call Cotton-tail?**

a) The Firecracker.

b) The Firestarter.

c) The Fire-breathing Dragon.

Answer

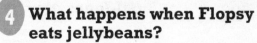

4 **What happens when Flopsy eats jellybeans?**

Answer

a) She feels a sudden urge to sing opera.

b) She falls asleep.

c) She goes completely bananas.

A TERRIBLY TRICKY TRUE OR FALSE

QUIZ

This quiz is for uber-fans only. Good luck!

TRUE or FALSE

1 Peter Rabbit lives near Derwentwater.

2 Cotton-tail is older than Flopsy.

3 Flopsy is younger than Mopsy.

4 Tom Kitten was put into a carrot cake.

5 Thomas McGregor always dreamed of owning his own toyshop. And now his dream has come true!

TRUE or FALSE

6 Barnabas once knew Peter Rabbit's father. ☐ ☐

7 Basil-Jones Publishing is based in Gloucester. ☐ ☐

8 Peter is a fierce, bad rabbit. ☐ ☐

9 Thomas is allergic to nuts. ☐ ☐

10 For each copy of Bea's book that is sold, 30% is donated to land preservation. ☐ ☐

SPEAK UP!

Match the character's name with a phrase they might say.

NIGEL BASIL-JONES
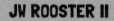

JW ROOSTER II

PIGLING BLAND

THOMAS

1 I don't like to overeat, you know. Mmm. Rose petals! Rice! Compost! Snort, snort, YUM.

....

2 Leave my tomatoes alone . . . OR ELSE.

....

3 I spy a bestseller! Look, over there! The one with the villainous rabbit!

....

4 It's MORNING. Wake up, wake up, wake up, wake up! NOW.

....

STAR RABBITS

Match the descriptions to the characters on this poster created by Nigel Basil-Jones!

PETER RABBIT

....

BENJAMIN BUNNY

....

MRS. TIGGY-WINKLE

....

THE DYNAMIC DUO   THE BAD SEED

THE WISE ONE   THE FIRECRACKER

THE BREAK-OUT ROLE

FLOPSY AND MOPSY

....

COTTON-TAIL

....

THE
THOMAS McGREGOR

He used to be grumpy and grouchy, but now he's met Bea, Thomas McGregor is a changed man! How much do you know about the new, cheery Thomas . . . ?

1 Thomas pretends to be really good at something. What?

Answer

a) Snooker.

b) Skateboarding.

c) Boxing.

2 What does Thomas contribute to Bea's book about Peter Rabbit?

Answer

a) He does the typesetting and the artisanal lithography, using a five-colour palette for the illustrations.

b) He glues the pages together.

c) He makes tea and coffee for Bea.

3 Thomas is always running out of . . . ?

Answer ☐

a) Semi-skimmed milk.

b) Tea.

c) Petrol.

4 What are Thomas's absolutely favourite things to grow – and eat – in the whole world?

Answer ☐

a) Cauliflowers.

b) Melons.

c) Tomatoes.

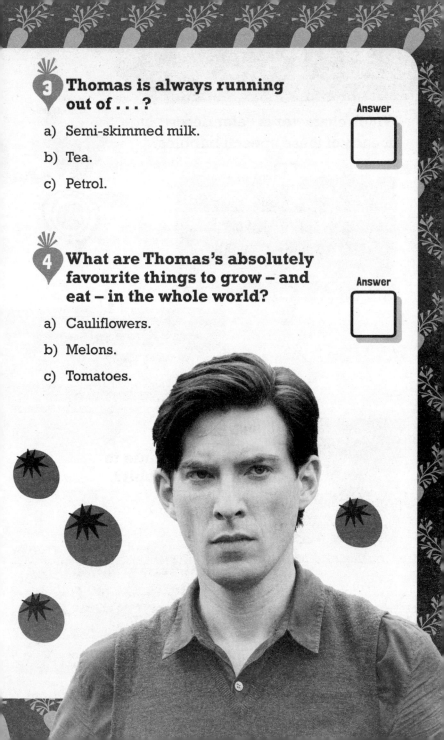

PETER SAYS . . .

Which character is Peter describing in each of these speech bubbles?

1

HE'S WISE AND HE'S SMART.
NO RABBIT COULD WISH
FOR A BETTER SIDEKICK.

....

2

SHE'S OLDER THAN MOPSY.
I THINK . . .

....

3

HE SINGS ON THE STREETS,
BUT HE DESERVES TO BE
ONSTAGE!

....

4

TO BEGIN WITH, I REALLY
DIDN'T LIKE HIM. NOW,
I'LL ADMIT THAT HE'S NOT
SUCH A BAD DAD.

....

A VERY DIFFICULT WORD SEARCH

Can you find these characters' names in probably the trickiest word search of all time? Good luck!

B	A	R	N	A	B	A	S	M	R	X	C
R	D	O	X	W	H	M	H	N	N	W	O
Q	A	G	F	L	O	P	S	Y	I	R	T
P	E	T	E	R	S	M	A	T	G	T	T
B	E	N	J	A	M	I	N	M	E	S	O
F	T	G	I	L	Q	U	L	H	L	U	N
K	H	C	H	M	P	E	T	E	M	S	T
G	O	M	R	O	O	S	T	E	R	M	A
O	M	P	K	N	D	Y	R	M	A	O	I
M	A	I	Q	B	Z	I	G	S	V	P	L
E	S	C	E	E	N	F	J	X	D	S	U
W	L	J	Z	A	M	T	L	K	B	Y	P

BARNABAS

BEA

BENJAMIN

COTTONTAIL

FLOPSY

MOPSY

NIGEL

PETER

ROOSTER

THOMAS

77

BENJAMIN BUNNY'S

QUIZ

It's Benjamin's turn to step into the spotlight! How much do you know about Peter Rabbit's seriously super sidekick?

 What colour is Benjamin's jacket?

a) Purple.

b) Brown.

c) Blue.

Answer

2 Benjamin and Peter are . . .

a) Brothers.

b) Cousins.

c) Casual acquaitances.

Answer

3 What is Benjamin full of?

a) Helpful advice and top tips.

b) Carrots.

c) Energy.

Answer

4 If Benjamin heard that Peter Rabbit was in danger, would he . . .

a) Think long and hard about the perfect rescue plan.

b) Wish that someone else would rescue him.

c) Go and rescue Peter AT ONCE.

Answer

TOWN OR COUNTRY?

Where do these characters live? In town or in the country? Draw a line to connect each character with their home.

TOWN

COUNTRY

BARNABAS

TOM KITTEN

COTTON-TAIL

FLOPSY

MOPSY

MITTENS

SAMUEL WHISKERS

PETER

SHOUT ALL ABOUT IT!

JW Rooster II has some amazing facts to share. The question is, which are cock-a-doodle-true and which are cock-a-doodle-false...?

1

PETER RABBIT WAS IN CHARGE OF THE WEDDING RING AT BEA'S WEDDING AND HE DIDN'T LOSE IT!

| TRUE | FALSE |

2

WINDERMERE IS IN AUSTRALIA!

| TRUE | FALSE |

3

PETER RABBIT IS PLANNING ON TRADING IN HIS SIGNATURE BLUE JACKET FOR AN ORANGE ONE!

| TRUE | FALSE |

4

BEA HAS PLANNED A 23-BOOK
SERIES FEATURING 109 CHARACTERS
BASED ON THE ANIMALS IN HER LIFE!

| TRUE | FALSE |

5

A ROOSTER'S COCK-A-DOODLE-DOO
IS MAGICALLY ABLE TO SWITCH ON
A SPRINKLER SYSTEM!
(But don't tell Rooster that.)

| TRUE | FALSE |

MOVIE MAGIC

Find 10 magical movie words in this word search.

L	X	B	O	O	K	S	D	L	C	J	F
A	F	T	O	M	A	T	O	E	S	L	I
K	S	R	Z	E	L	F	G	S	B	N	R
E	N	H	L	Z	D	P	L	Z	I	A	E
D	E	J	P	U	I	Q	O	X	L	L	C
I	A	G	O	O	C	X	U	B	L	A	R
S	K	W	T	R	K	E	C	O	B	V	A
T	E	L	S	B	E	L	E	L	O	A	C
R	R	D	C	I	N	T	S	H	A	T	K
I	S	N	M	L	S	A	T	S	R	O	E
C	W	P	E	T	E	R	E	K	D	R	R
T	Y	G	Q	I	A	U	R	P	L	Y	M

TOMATOES	BOOKS
FIRECRACKER	BILLBOARD
GLOUCESTER	SNEAKERS
LAKE DISTRICT	DICKENS
PETER	LAVATORY

CROSSWORD

How much can you remember about the movie?
Test your knowledge with this crossword, then
unscramble the name of one of its stars using
the letters in the shaded squares.

ACROSS:
1   Who is the star of the movie? (5)
3   What town do the family visit? (10)
5   Which foxy character's name rhymes with 'pod'? (2, 3)

DOWN:
2   What kind of bird wakes the farm animals each day? (7)
4   Is Cotton-tail the youngest or oldest triplet? (8)
6   What is Mr. McGregor's favourite vegetable? (8)

WHICH RABBIT ARE YOU?

Which rabbit are you most like? Answer these super scientific questions to find out!

1 **There's a box of scrumptious chocolates in the kitchen and there's no one around. What do you do?**

a) Peek inside, decide that you're just going to eat one or two. Then three or four. And oops, they're all gone.

b) Go and ask someone if you can help yourself.

c) Gobble the lot in five seconds flat.

Answer

2 **Which description fits you best?**

a) Good-looking, friendly, quick-witted and oh-so-charming.

b) Caring, kind, wise and always ready to help.

c) Daring, dangerous and up for a challenge.

Answer

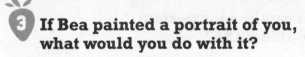

3 If Bea painted a portrait of you, what would you do with it?

a) Hang it over the mantelpiece so that everyone can see it.

b) Put it in your room, so you can see it.

c) Sell it. You'd make a fortune!

Answer

4 What's your best subject at school?

a) PE – you are so sporty.

b) English – you love settling down with a good book.

c) Maths – you're pretty good at working things out.

Answer

5 What would your perfect day out include?

a) Hundreds of rides in a dizzyingly exciting theme park.

b) A tour of cake shops and art galleries.

c) Bowling followed by an all-you-can-eat buffet.

Answer

6 Choose an outfit for a fancy dress party!

a) A superhero.

b) A chef.

c) A prisoner with a stripy uniform.

Answer

7 What is your signature dance move?

a) Spinning on your head.

b) A pirouette.

c) Popping and locking.

Answer

 8 What's your favourite colour?

a) Sky blue.

b) Brown.

c) Deepest, darkest grey.

Answer

IF YOU ANSWERED MOSTLY...

a) You are cheeky and loveable, like Peter Rabbit.

b) You are wise and helpful, like Benjamin.

c) You are super sneaky, like Barnabas.

QUIZ ANSWERS

PAGE 12: WEDDING WHEEL

_ A _ M I L Y _

F A M I L Y

PAGE 13: CHARACTER CONFUSION

BENJAMIN

PAGES 16–17: ODD ONE OUT

1: C   4: B
2: A   5: C
3: D   6: A

PAGES 22–23: BOTHER IN GLOUCESTER

PAGE 25: BOUNCING BUNNIES

7   4   6   5   3

PAGE 32: MYSTERY MAZE

PAGE 33: IN THE SHADE

1. Barnabas
2. Tom Kitten
3. Mittens
4. Samuel Whiskers

PAGE 46: RADISH RUN

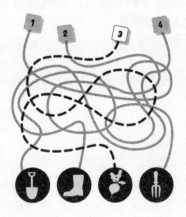

PAGE 50: THE PERFECTLY HUGE PETER RABBIT QUIZ

1.B 2.C 3.A 4.B 5.C 6.C 7.A 8.B

PAGES 54–55: WHAT'S MISSING?

Meet Peter Rabbit! He's ......**cheeky**......,
he's funny and he's terribly good at pinching
......**carrots**...... . Unfortunately, he's not that
great at recognizing when others are telling
......**fibs**...... .

Take ......**Barnabas**......, for instance. He's
......**rotten**......, through and through.
But he convinces poor Peter to swap
the beautiful ......**countryside**...... for a life
of crime in the big ......**city**...... .

And before he knows it, Peter is involved
in a ......**plot**...... to steal a huge amount
of produce from a farmers' ......**market**...... .
Will he see the ......**error**...... of his ways
in time? Or will it be too late . . . ?

PAGES 56–57: BEA'S QUIZ

1. C
2. C
3. A
4. B

PAGES 58–59: BENJAMIN'S TOP TIPS

1. True
2. False
3. True
4. False
5. True
6. False
7. False
8. False
9. True
10. False

PAGES 60–61: NIGEL BASIL-JONES

Meet Nigel Basil-Jones, the publisher! He is
very handsome and super ......**successful**...... .
His fancy office is ......**gigantic**......, its shelves
lined with many, many ......**books**...... .

Nigel is incredibly charming to all of his
......**authors**...... . Take the delightful
......**Bea**......, for example. He makes
sure to ......**kiss**...... her hand when he
meets her.

And he creates a wonderful area where Bea's
......**rabbit**...... family can ......**relax**...... .
As Nigel is so enormously ......**confident**......, he
is sure that he can turn Bea's new book
into a ......**bestseller**...... . All she has to do is
change it, just a little.

PAGE 62: PLOT TWIST!

1. False 2. False 3. False 4. False
5. True 6. True 7. False 8. False 9. True

PAGES 64–65: FLOPSY, MOPSY AND COTTON-TAIL

1. A   3. A
2. B   4. C

PAGES 66–67: A TERRIBLY TRICKY TRUE OR FALSE

1. False 2. False 3. False 4. False 5. True
6. False 7. True 8. False 9. False 10. True

PAGES 68–69: SPEAK UP!

1. Pigling Bland
2. Thomas
3. Nigel Basil-Jones
4. JW Rooster II

PAGES 70–71: STAR RABBITS

1. THE BAD SEED (Peter)
2. THE WISE ONE (Benjamin)
3. THE BREAK-OUT ROLE (Mrs. Tiggy-winkle)
4. THE DYNAMIC DUO (Flopsy and Mopsy)
5. THE FIRECRACKER (Cotton-tail)

PAGES 72–73: THE THOMAS McGREGOR QUIZ

1. C   3. C
2. A   4. C

PAGES 74–75: PETER SAYS ...

1. Benjamin
2. Flopsy
3. Johnny Town-mouse
4. Thomas
5. Barnabas

PAGES 76–77: A VERY DIFFICULT WORD SEARCH

```
B A R N A B A S M R X C
R D O X W H M H N N W O
O A G F L O P S Y I R T
P E T E R S M A T G T T
B E N J A M I N M E S O
F T G I L O U L H L U N
K H C H M P E T E N S T
G O M R O O S T E R M A
O M P K N D Y R M A O I
M A I O B Z I G S V P L
E S C E E N F J X D S U
W L J Z A M T L K B Y P
```

PAGES 78–79: BENJAMIN BUNNY'S QUIZ

1. B   3. A
2. B   4. C

PAGES 80–81: TOWN OR COUNTRY?

TOWN
Barnabas
Samuel Whiskers
Tom Kitten
Mittens

COUNTRY
Peter Rabbit
Flopsy
Mopsy
Cotton-tail

PAGES 82–83: SHOUT ALL ABOUT IT!

1. True
2. False
3. False
4. True
5. False

PAGE 84: MOVIE MAGIC

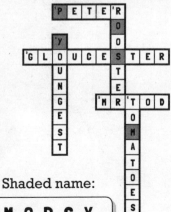

PAGE 85: CROSSWORD

Shaded name:

M O P S Y